Unlock the Door

Now is the time to discover
the truth about your life

ERIN REID

WESTBOW
P R E S S
A DIVISION OF THOMAS NELSON

ISBN: 978-1-4497-4532-5 (e)
ISBN: 978-1-4497-4531-8 (sc)
Library of Congress Control Number: 2012906020

WestBow Press books may be ordered through booksellers or by contacting:
WestBow Press
A Division of Thomas Nelson
1663 Liberty Drive
Bloomington, IN 47403
www.westbowpress.com
1-(866) 928-1240

Printed in the United States of America
WestBow Press rev. date: 4/24/2012

Introduction

Deep in every heart is a curiosity. Who am I? How did I get here? Why am I here? It is an age-old question, but somehow the answers often remain buried. In this book I endeavor to unlock the door and switch on the light to the truth that may have otherwise remained a mystery. The truth is out there, and the truth *will* set you free.

The Lord has given me a heavy burden for the world's lost and broken souls. He has given me a clear word to write this book. He has shown me his heart for his lost children and given me an anointing to write through his Holy Spirit. It is my hope and prayer that the words in these chapters will be received, and the lost souls will discover their destiny in the kingdom of heaven.

Contents

Introduction   v

Chapter 1   Who Is God?   1

Chapter 2   Satan and Temptation   27

Chapter 3   Heaven and Hell   43

Chapter 4   Jesus' Return and the End Times   51

Chapter 5   Judgment Day   63

Chapter 6   God's Plan for Your Life   67

Chapter 7   Salvation   75

Father's Heart   81

About the Author   85

*My brothers and sisters, if one of you wanders away
from the truth, and someone helps that person come
back, remember this: Anyone who brings a sinner
back from the wrong way will save that sinner's soul
from death and will cause many sins to be forgiven.*

(James 5:19–20 *NCV*)

CHAPTER 1

Who Is God?

To start our journey, I need to introduce you to the one who is at the center of everything. He is the one upon whom everything in our world, our history, and our entire universe is built. He is God, and without God there would be nothing.

I cannot describe to you in human words how wonderful, how awesome, and how enormous God is. No human description can ever convey the complexity, wonder, and love of our Lord. I could write all day and still not come slightly close enough to portraying an image in your mind of who God is. He is too enormous for our minds to contemplate. He is simply indescribable.

We have probably all had different perceptions and imaginings of who we think God is. All we can do is turn to the Bible, God's own Word, to see who he says he is. The more you seek to learn more about God, the more chance you have that he will reveal himself to you. You may feel him in your heart, you may feel more aware of his presence as you read this book, or you may just feel a knowing deep inside that he is the true God. Let yourself experience God's presence and voice as he reveals himself to you through these pages.

The Father God Is Eternal

In the beginning there was God. Before the beginning there was God. God has always been and will always be. God is eternal; he is not limited to time. God is infinite; he is not contained by space.

*In the beginning God... (*Genesis 1:1 NCV)

Our human mind struggles to grasp the idea that time and space as we know it began at an actual point; before that beginning was the infinite and eternal God. God was there forever and ever before time and will be there forever and ever in the future. He has no beginning and no end. He is eternal.

God Is the Creator

With one decision, God created the heavens and the earth, and history as we know it began. Existence became time, and time became measurable. God's voice commanded the universe and the earth into existence. By his might he created day and night, water and air, land and animals, and trees and fish. He carved the canyons and valleys, formed the mountains and the rivers, and placed each animal and creature where it belonged on the earth. God saw that this was good.

> *Then God said, "Let us make human beings in our image and likeness. And let them rule over the fish in the sea and the birds in the sky, over the tame animals, over all the earth, and over all the small crawling animals on the earth."*

> *So God created human beings in his image. In the image of God he created them. He created them male and female. God blessed them and said, "Have many children and grow in number. Fill the earth and be its master. Rule over the fish in the sea and over the birds in the sky and over every living thing that moves on the earth."* (Genesis 1:26–28 NCV)

God made humans in his likeness and image. Yet he gave each of us an individual identity and uniqueness. He loved us so much he made us like him, so we could understand him and enjoy a close relationship with him. He made us that we would reflect the very nature of God himself and live in love on the earth he created for us. He gave us responsibility and dominion over all the rest of creation, and he told us to rule over every living thing on the earth. God created the earth perfect for humans to enjoy and to enjoy close relationship with him, but as I discuss in later chapters, God's perfection was messed up. God's intention for us was to live in close relationship with him and with each other.

Notice in the Scripture above God says, "Let us make human beings in our image and likeness." Who, then, is the *us*? God is talking about himself, the Father; Jesus, his Son; and the person of the Holy Spirit. You see, God is made up of three beings, but they are all one eternal God.

God Is Love

As 1 John 4:8 (NIV) says, "Whoever does not love does not know God, because God is love."

God created the heavens and earth out of love. He created us in his image out of love. God is love in every way. He loves us as his children. He loves every one of us no matter who we are or what we have done. His love is never failing and never ending. We can do nothing to make him love us any less. He has always loved us, even before the beginning of time. He knew us before the earth began. He had us planned before we were born, and he knew us and loved us.

God is an all-knowing God. He knows everything about everything. His knowledge is eternal, his love is eternal, and his plan is eternal. God is everywhere at the same time. We can go nowhere to escape him.

Jesus: The Son of God

In the Beginning was the Word,
and the Word was with God, and the
Word was God. He was with God in the
beginning.

> *All things were made by him, and*
> *nothing was made without him. In him*
> *there was life, and that life was the light of*
> *all people. The light shines in the darkness,*
> *and the darkness has not overpowered it.*
> (John 1:1–5 NCV)

As Luke 19:10 (NCV) says, "The Son of Man came to find lost people and save them." Before we meet Jesus, we are lost. Our souls are lost because we were created to live in fellowship and friendship with our Creator. We are lost and separated from God because of our sin. Sin is the separation between what God says is right and our own selfish will. But there is good news: a little more than two thousand years ago, a Savior was born. God sent his only son, Jesus, to earth to save all his children from their sins. I assume we all know the story behind Christmas, and I don't mean the story of Santa Claus. Jesus was born 100 percent man and 100 percent God. He was born to the Virgin Mary, who agreed to raise the boy—the Son of God.

> *This is how the birth of Jesus Christ*
> *came about: His mother Mary was pledged*
> *to be married to Joseph, but before they*
> *came together, she was found to be with*
> *child through the Holy Spirit. Because*

Joseph her husband was a righteous man and did not want to expose her to public disgrace, he had in mind to divorce her quietly.

But after he had considered this, an angel of the Lord appeared to him in a dream and said, "Joseph son of David, do not be afraid to take Mary home as your wife, because what is conceived in her is from the Holy Spirit. She will give birth to a son, and you are to give him the name Jesus, because he will save his people from their sins."

All this took place to fulfill what the Lord had said through the prophet: "The virgin will be with child and will give birth to a son, and they will call him Immanuel"— which means, "God with us."

When Joseph woke up, he did what the angel of the Lord had commanded him and took Mary home as his wife. But he had no union with her until she gave birth to a son. And he gave him the name Jesus. (Matthew 1:18–25 NIV 1984)

It is quite easy for the world to get confused about the true meaning behind Christmas. Getting caught up in the sparkle, pretty lights, presents, and plum pudding is easy, but what are we missing? We are missing out on the birth of our Savior, Jesus Christ, whom God put on this earth to become a sacrifice for our sins and to bridge the gap from our sin to our eternal life. "For all have sinned and fall short of the glory of God" (Romans 3:23 NIV).

Because of our sin, and all humans have sinned, God wanted to save us so he sent his Son, Jesus, to earth to live amongst us and teach us his way of life. God wanted us to live in fellowship with him again, just as he intended for us to live from the beginning. The only way we could be free to fellowship with God was if we were free of our sin. God needed a plan to wipe out all our sin and give us access to a close relationship with him. In order to do this, God made Jesus a sacrifice for our sin. Jesus was to die on a cross and become sin in our place, so we would be set free. "Jesus is the only One who can save people. No one else in the world is able to save us" (Acts 4:12 NCV).

God the Son was born and lived on this earth as a sinless man. He gave up his human life to save ours. His death was the only acceptable payment for our sin. Jesus is our only way to God the Father and to heaven and eternal life. He died so that when we get to heaven, we will become eternal beings like him, and our souls will live forever in heaven with God. Without Jesus, we are spiritually dead.

In reply Jesus declared, "I tell you the truth, no one can see the kingdom of God unless he is born again" (John 3:3 NIV 1984). At Easter we remember what Jesus did for us on the cross. Easter is not about the Easter Bunny or chocolate eggs; it's about the sacrificial death of Jesus Christ on the cross to take away the sin of the world. We have the access to new life, to being born again. Our old, sinful selves have died, and our new life in Christ has begun. We can leave behind our sinful selves and take up our new lives in Jesus. He gives us new hope and a new beginning.

Most people think if they are good they will go to heaven, and a wonderful existence awaits them after they die. Jesus tells us that that is not true. Only one sort of people will make it to heaven. Jesus himself said, "I am the way, the truth, and the life. No one comes to the Father except through Me." (John 14:6 NIV 1984)

When we believe in our hearts that Jesus is who he says he is, and we believe that he did come to earth to save us from our sins, we become *born again.* In order to be born again, we must make Jesus our Savior and Lord of our life by giving our life back to him in exchange for our eternal life. When we give Jesus our life and are willing to give up our sinful life, then Jesus will make us into a new creation in his likeness. We now have Jesus living in our heart, and we become a born-again Christian. We now have eternal life; when we die from this life on earth, we have eternity waiting for us in heaven. Our soul is eternal and will live forever. If we don't believe in Jesus; however, we remain separated from God by our sin and will spend eternity in hell. We will learn about the reality of heaven and hell in the coming chapters.

> *For God so loved the world that he gave his one and only Son, that whoever believes in him shall not perish but have eternal life. For God did not send his Son into the world to condemn the world, but to save the world through him.* (John 3:16–17 NIV)

> *Jesus Christ said: "Ask and it will be given to you; seek and you will find; knock and the door will be opened to you. For everyone who asks receives; he who seeks finds; and to him who knocks, the door will be opened."* (Matthew 7:7–8 NIV 1984)

All we have to do is simply ask to have Jesus as our Lord and Savior to receive eternal life in heaven. Remember, God is everywhere all the time and knows everything, so when we talk to him he can hear us. He is all knowing, so he can also hear our thoughts and knows when we speak to him in our mind, no matter where we are.

When Jesus walked on earth in his human body, he was 100 percent man and 100 percent God. Because he was man, he was subject to all the temptations that we have. Because he was also God, he was perfect in his nature and overcame the temptations of evil. Many times in Jesus' life the Devil tried to tempt him, but because he was God and had the Spirit of God living in him, he had the power to overcome temptation. He also knew Satan all too well.

Jesus was God on earth; therefore, he had the power of God. Jesus was known to perform many miracles. He was very popular in his day, and everyone wanted to get a glimpse of him and see the wonders that he performed. He healed the sick, the blind, and the demon possessed. He calmed storms and walked on water. He taught that we too have access to this power. Through faith, we have the access of his power and his grace. The power that Jesus used to walk on water and heal the sick is the same power that we have access to today. All we need is faith.

> *Therefore, since we have been justified*
> *through faith, we have peace with God*
> *through our Lord Jesus Christ, through*
> *whom we have gained access by faith into*
> *this grace in which we now stand. And we*
> *rejoice in the hope of the glory of God.*
> (Romans 5:1–2 NIV 1984)

I love this verse. We have gained access by faith into the grace or *power* of God.

> *The Lord said, If your faith were the*
> *size of a mustard seed, you could say to this*
> *mulberry tree, 'Dig yourself up and plant*
> *yourself in the sea,' and it would obey you.*
> (Luke 17:6 NCV)

> *A large crowd followed Jesus and*
> *pushed very close around him. Among them*
> *was a woman who had been bleeding for*
> *twelve years. She had suffered very much*
> *from many doctors and had spent all the*
> *money she had, but instead of improving,*
> *she was getting worse. When the woman*
> *heard about Jesus, she came up behind*
> *him in the crowd and touched his coat. She*
> *thought, "If I can just touch his clothes,*

*I will be healed." Instantly her bleeding
stopped, and she felt in her body that she
was healed from her disease.*

*At once Jesus felt power go out from him.
So he turned around in the crowd and asked,
"Who touched my clothes?" His followers
said, "Look at how many people are pushing
against you! And you ask, 'Who touched me?'"*

*But Jesus continued looking around
to see who had touched him. The woman,
knowing that she was healed, came and
fell at Jesus' feet. Shaking with fear, she
told him the whole truth. Jesus said to her,
"Dear woman, you are made well because
you believed. Go in peace; be healed of your
disease."* (Mark 5:24-34 NCV)

*Then they came to Jericho. As Jesus
and his disciples, together with a large
crowd, were leaving the city, a blind
man, Bartimaeus (which means "son of
Timaeus"), was sitting by the roadside
begging. When he heard that it was Jesus of
Nazareth, he began to shout, "Jesus, Son of
David, have mercy on me!"*

> *Many rebuked him and told him to be*
> *quiet, but he shouted all the more, "Son of*
> *David, have mercy on me!"*
>
> *Jesus stopped and said, "Call him."*
>
> *So they called to the blind man, "Cheer*
> *up! On your feet! He's calling you."*
> *Throwing his cloak aside, he jumped to his*
> *feet and came to Jesus.*
>
> *"What do you want me to do for you?"*
> *Jesus asked him.*
>
> *The blind man said, "Rabbi, I want to see."*
>
> *"Go," said Jesus, "your faith has*
> *healed you." Immediately he received his*
> *sight and followed Jesus along the road.*
> (Mark 10:46–52 NIV)

Whenever Jesus performed a miracle or healed someone, it was always through faith—the faith of Jesus and the faith of the person receiving the miracle. Power is released when we have faith.

What is faith? Faith is the complete trust or confidence in something or someone; faith is the confident belief or trust in a person, idea, or thing that is not based on proof. So, as a believer of Christ, I have faith that Jesus is Lord and has the power to heal and save me from my sins. This faith grants me access into his grace.

What is grace? Grace is our undeserved favor from God. Grace is our empowerment to do God's will. Grace gives power to say no to sin. God freely gives grace to us that we might escape the stronghold and corruption of sin and fulfill his will in our life. God has provided us with the grace and power we need for our daily lives and for holy living. Jesus is willing to share his power of supernatural strength so that we can be like him in our thoughts, attitudes, love, faith, and purity. This grace will empower us to continue his mission of destroying the Devil's works and setting others free from Satan. All we need to do is receive the free gift of grace, through faith. Ephesians 2:8 NIV says, "For it is by grace you have been saved, through faith—and this is not from yourselves, it is the gift of God."

Jesus was thirty when he started his public ministry. Before that he worked as a carpenter with his earthly father. His public ministry only lasted a couple of years. In that time he gathered twelve disciples and taught them through his teachings. His teachings consisted of using parables, metaphors, allegories, sayings, proverbs, and a few direct sermons. His life and his teachings are all recorded in the Bible, which his disciples and close followers wrote. We know the life and teachings of our Lord through the Bible and through first-hand accounts and witnesses.

This was the first coming of Christ. The second coming of Christ is when Jesus will return to earth to collect all his children and raise them up with him into heaven. This second coming is also known as the *rapture.*

Pontius Pilate arrested and sentenced Jesus to be whipped and executed on a cross after only a couple of years or so into Jesus' ministry. These horrific events took place as a public display. Jesus was innocent and a sinless man, but because he claimed he was the Messiah and indeed the Son of God, he was looked upon by many as a liar and a crazy man.

The proof that Jesus was the Son of God is in his death and resurrection. Any man can die, and in that time in history many men who broke the law were sentenced to death by hanging on a cross. But not every man can die and three days later, after being

buried, rise to life again in his new heavenly body.
Jesus was nailed to a cross and hung there from 9 a.m.
until 3 p.m. Then in the last hour he gave up his spirit
and died.

> *And when Jesus cried out again in a*
> *loud voice, he gave up his spirit. At that*
> *moment the curtain of the temple was torn*
> *in two from top to bottom. The earth shook*
> *and the rocks split. The tombs broke open*
> *and the bodies of many holy people who*
> *had died were raised to life. They came out*
> *of the tombs, and after Jesus' resurrection*
> *they went into the holy city and appeared to*
> *many people.*
>
> *When the centurion and those with him*
> *who were guarding Jesus saw the earth and*
> *all that had happened, they were terrified, and*
> *exclaimed, "Surely he was the Son of God!"*
> (Matthew 27:50–54 NIV)

His body was taken to be buried in a new tomb close
by in a garden. He was prepared for burial and wrapped
in cloth. Then a large stone that covered the doorway to
the tomb was placed in front of the opening. Jesus was
left inside and laid to rest.

After the Sabbath, at dawn on the first day of the week, Mary Magdalene and the other Mary went to look at the tomb.

There was a violent earthquake, for an angel of the Lord came down from heaven and, going to the tomb, rolled back the stone and sat on it. His appearance was like lightning, and his clothes were white as snow. The guards were so afraid of him that they shook and became like dead men.

The angel said to the women, "Do not be afraid, for I know that you are looking for Jesus, who was crucified. He is not here; he has risen, just as he said. Come and see the place where he lay. Then go quickly and tell his disciples: 'He has risen from the dead and is going ahead of you into Galilee. There you will see him.' Now I have told you."

So the women hurried away from the tomb, afraid yet filled with joy, and ran to tell his disciples. Suddenly Jesus met them. "Greetings," he said. They came to him, clasped his feet and worshipped him. Then Jesus said to them, "Do not be afraid. Go

*and tell my brothers to go to Galilee; there
they will see me."* (Matthew 28:1–10 NIV)

Jesus appeared to many people during a span of
forty days after his resurrection.

> *On the evening of that first day of the
> week, when the disciples were together, with
> the doors locked for fear of the Jews, Jesus
> came and stood among them and said, "Peace
> be with you!" After he said this, he showed
> them his hands and side. The disciples were
> overjoyed when the saw the Lord.*
>
> *Again Jesus said, "Peace be with you!
> As the Father has sent me, I am sending
> you." And with that he breathed on them
> and said, "Receive the Holy Spirit."* (John
> 20:19–22 NIV 1984)

Jesus promised that the Father would send the Holy
Spirit as our helper and counsellor after Jesus returned
to heaven after the forty days.

> *"Now I am going to him who sent me, yet
> none of you asks me, 'Where are you going?'
> Because I have said these things, you are filled*

with grief. But I tell you the truth: It is for your good that I am going away. Unless I go away, the Counsellor will not come to you; but if I go, I will send him to you. When he comes, he will convict the world of guilt in regard to sin and righteousness and judgement: in regard to sin, because men do not believe in me; in regard to righteousness, because I am going to the Father, where you can see me no longer; and in regard to judgement, because the prince of this world now stands condemned.

"I have much more to say to you, more than you can now bear. But when he, the Spirit of truth, comes, he will guide you into all truth. He will not speak on his own; he will speak only what he hears, and he will tell you what is yet to come. He will bring glory to me by taking from what is mine and making it known to you. All that belongs to the Father is mine. That is why I said the Spirit will take from what is mine and make it known to you.

"In a little while you will see me no more, and then after a little while you will see me."
(John 16:5–16 NIV 1984)

After the forty days, and after Jesus had promised the Holy Spirit, he descended into the sky and into heaven, and we know he will return. Acts 1:11 NIV 1984 says, "This same Jesus, who has been taken from you into heaven, will come back in the same way you have seen him go into heaven."

Jesus is now in heaven with our Father. He will remain there until he comes back again, the same way he was taken into heaven.

The Holy Spirit

The realness of God, living through us and in us, is just as real as Jesus is, alive and living in heaven. The same Spirit who lived in Jesus when he walked the earth is alive and living in us, just as God had promised. When we become believers of Jesus, God gives us his Holy Spirit to be our helper. He will give us spiritual gifts for use in ministry and power to live Godly lives.

The Holy Spirit is God; he is a person equal in every way with God the Father and God the Son. He is not a ghost or a force. The Holy Spirit's mission and purpose is to reveal Jesus. Just as it is Jesus' mission to reveal the Father, and the Father's mission to send Jesus and the Holy Spirit so we can come to him. All three are separate, but all are one God. They are in perfect harmony.

Although the Holy Spirit has the same characteristics of God, he has specific roles and functions in our lives. The Bible shows us that the Spirit of truth is our guide.

> *But when he, the Spirit of truth, comes,*
> *he will guide you into all truth. He will not*
> *speak on his own; he will speak only what*
> *he hears, and he will tell you what is yet to*
> *come.* (John 16:13 NIV 1984)

In John 14:26 (NIV 1984), we learn that the Holy Spirit is our Counsellor and Teacher. "But the Counsellor, the Holy Spirit, whom the Father will send in my name, will teach you all things and will remind you of everything I have said to you."

In 1 Corinthians 3:16 (NIV 1984), we see that the Holy Spirit lives inside us. "Don't you know that you yourselves are God's temple and that God's Spirit lives in you?"

In Acts 1:8 (NIV 1984), we understand where our power comes from. "But you will receive power when the Holy Spirit comes on you."

In Romans 8:14 (NIV 1984), we understand where our direction comes from: "those who are led by the Spirit of God are sons of God."

In Romans 8:26 (NIV 1984), we learn that the Holy Spirit is there for us in times of weakness: "In the same way, the Spirit helps us in our weakness. We do not know what we ought to pray for, but the Spirit himself intercedes for us with groans that words cannot express."

Living in the Spirit

So I say, live by the Spirit, and you not gratify the desires of the sinful nature. For the sinful nature desires what is contrary to the Spirit, and the Spirit what is contrary to the sinful nature. They are in conflict with each other, so that you do not do what you want. But if you are led by the Spirit, you are not under law. (Galatians 5: 16–18 NIV 1984)

Christians are called to live their lives in the Holy Spirit. Those who do don't give in easily to sinful desires. Living in the Spirit is a sure way to stay on track as a Christian and to live closely in the purpose God has for you. Jesus sent the Holy Spirit to live in us as our helper and our guide. He will show us the right way to live, and he will direct our path.

> *But the fruit of the Spirit is love, joy,*
> *peace, patience, kindness, goodness,*
> *faithfulness, gentleness, and self-control.*
> *Against such things there is no law. Those*
> *who belong to Christ Jesus have crucified*
> *the sinful nature with its passions and*
> *desires. Since we live by the Spirit, let*
> *us keep in step with the Spirit. Let us not*
> *become conceited, provoking and envying*
> *each other.*
> (Galatians 5:22–26 NIV 1984)

Those who have the Lord Jesus as their Savior and who have received the Holy Spirit and walk in Him will be recognized as having the 'fruits of the Spirit'. A true Christian has these nine visible attributes. They are not just individual 'fruits,' but rather one ninefold 'fruit' that characterizes all who truly walk in the Holy Spirit. They are love, joy, peace, patience, kindness, goodness, faithfulness, gentleness, and self-control. God's children who are walking in the Spirit will produce these fruits in their transformed life in replace of the selfish desires they once had.

The Holy Spirit is God's way of always being with us. He said, "I will never leave you nor forsake you." After you receive the Holy Spirit and accept Jesus as your Lord and Savior and live in the Spirit, he will never leave you. You may stray far from him at times, but you can be sure that he never strays away from you. Having Him live right inside of you, renewing and transforming you into the creation he destined you to be, is the most exciting and rewarding part of your journey with God.

CHAPTER 2

Satan and Temptation

Satan is the Hebrew transliteration of the word *adversary,* the enemy of God and man. Satan is a liar, he is a thief, and we call him the Devil.

If you are reading this book for the first time, and you do not have much previous knowledge about God and Satan, you may be feeling a little overwhelmed at the moment. You have gone through life thinking that how you are living your life is normal. You are about to discover that forces are out there that you cannot see who are at war with each other.

God exists and so does Satan. A war between good and evil is being fought right in front of you. Satan and his demons are real, and they are at work in your life. But have hope, God can overcome evil and save you from its wickedness. My mission in writing this book is to open your eyes to the truth, so that the Devil will no longer have you deceived. Let me teach you some things about Satan so that you can see the truth more clearly.

God first created Satan as a guardian cherub angel. He covered the throne of God in heaven. He was the model of perfection, full of wisdom and perfect in beauty. But his heart became proud because of his beauty.

Satan became arrogant because of his splendor, and decided that he wanted to sit on a throne higher than God. Satan's pride led to his fall. Because of Satan's sinful pride, God barred Satan from heaven and created a fiery destiny—Hell—for Satan and the other fallen angels who decided to follow him. God didn't intend for his children to go to hell but sadly those who choose to ignore the call of God and follow after Satan will end up in hell with him. And hell is for eternity.

Even though Satan was cast out of heaven, he still seeks to elevate his throne above God. He counterfeits all that God does, hoping to gain the world's worship and encourage opposition to God's kingdom. Satan is the ultimate source behind every false cult and world religion. Satan will do anything and everything in his power to oppose God and those who follow God.

However, Satan's destiny is sealed—an eternity in the lake of fire.

> *And the devil, who deceived them, was*
> *thrown into the lake of burning sulphur,*
> *where the beast and false prophet had been*
> *thrown. They will be tormented day and*
> *night forever and ever.* (Revelation 20:10
> NIV 1984)

Satan was in the garden of Eden when God created Adam and Eve. He deceived them into partaking in evil, which God had warned them not to do. Satan seduced and tempted Eve to sin, and then Eve also persuaded Adam to sin, which was the beginning of the fall of humanity. At this point, sin entered the world and entered the human race, God's children.

Satan couldn't stand God having his own precious children, so he plotted a way to deceive them. Satan wants to destroy everything that belongs to God and claim it for himself. He still seeks to destroy us today. His desire is to stop people from coming to know God and to deceive God's children into turning their back on God. Satan wants to be our god, and he'll do everything in his power to try and make that happen.

Just like God has a plan and destiny for your life, the Devil also has his own plan for your life. His plan is to steal, kill, and destroy everything good in your life. He wants to destroy your faith, your happiness, and your joy. He comes after your family, your friendships, your job, your finances, and your health; he wants to ruin anything he can get his hands on.

The Devil is very smart and cunning in the way he steals from people. He has been around since the world began, and he has us figured out. He knows that if he steals from us outright, his actions will be recognized. He is very careful to steal from people in such a deceptive way that we will often not even realize until his evil goal is accomplished.

The Devil's best way of getting us is through our mind. Satan injects thoughts into our mind to steal our peace, our joy, and even our beliefs. He tries his best to keep us bound in negative thoughts and depression. He wants us to struggle through life, feeling defeated and powerless. He makes us feel like life's victims. He'll bring debt, sickness, depression, busyness, misery, and stress into our lives to stop us from pursuing our God-given destinies.

The Devil is very good at getting you to think negatively about yourself; therefore, making your life's outcomes negative. A lot of women and men struggle with self esteem issues, which is a great way for the Devil to get inside your head. If you're thinking negative thoughts about yourself, it's a sure sign that the Devil has a hold of you. You need to be aware that these thoughts are from the Devil, the master liar, and they hold no truth in your life. The Lord made you unique, and he made you *you* for a reason. God doesn't make mistakes. He designed you individually and crafted each of his children into his master plan. You have a purpose and a plan for being here. Everyone is different and everyone is special. We each have a unique purpose and destiny designed for the Kingdom of God and his will. We just have to seek God, and he will show us our gifts and talents. Each one of our lives is created for extraordinary feats. We were not designed for ordinary, everyday living. We were designed for extraordinary living—full of abundance, purpose, and *life*.

As John 10:10 (NIV 1984) says, "The thief comes only to steal and kill and destroy; I have come that they may have life, and have it to the full." The Devil wants to steal our joy, kill our dreams, and destroy our faith. But Jesus came to save us, so we can have life and life to the fullest.

Temptation V's Sin

Temptation is a desire to do something or a prompting to take part in something that is of the Devil. But you need to know that temptation is *not* sin. Being tempted in itself is not sin. Sin occurs when you give in to temptation. Temptation does not come from God. God will never tempt his children. Temptation comes from Satan. Satan has a plan to destroy God's purpose in life, and he will use temptation to stop God's children from fulfilling their dreams and purposes.

Satan uses temptation to deceive us into doing wrong and to lead us away from the destiny that God has for us. Satan is very crafty and has become adept at temping us. He gets to know our weaknesses and uses our interests to twist and deceive us into falling into temptation. For a person who doesn't know Jesus and is trying to go through life the best he or she knows how, Satan has him or her snagged in a deadly trap. Satan likes to hold his prisoners captive there. By using temptation and lies, Satan has them thinking that what they are doing and how they are living is normal.

Satan uses many temptations to capture his targets. Here we discuss a few of the more common ones in our society, but you need to understand that many more exist that you will think of. The best thing to help you overcome temptation is to be aware. Always have your eyes and ears open and guard your heart. Remember that Satan is at war with God for your heart, and he will try anything to get you away from knowing the *truth* of salvation.

Satan gets what he sets out to achieve through temptation and deceit. He uses all sorts of lies to deceive us into following him. Homosexuality, abortion, sexual sin, lust, greed, are gossip are all some of the ways he tempts us into following him. Non-Christians are blinded to the truth, so they don't think that anything is wrong with these things. Satan has control over their mind. This is Satan's deceitful way of making people worship him. They think in their mind that what they are doing is acceptable, but it's not. It is sin, and sin leads to eternal death.

The media, including television, radio, the Internet, and movies, is a huge advantage point for Satan. It is full of lies, deceit, sex, scandal, and sin of every kind. Billions of people tune into some sort of media outlet every day. The media outlets repetitively play these sinful messages over and over in people's minds. People see in the media that these messages are okay and that they're normal, natural, and everyday life, but they're *not!* The media is lying to you. The different media outlets are the Devil's playground and a sure way of him entering temptation into your mind and into your life.

Think of how much influence music and video clips have on a young person's life. These videos show gangster rap songs, full of hatred and racism, with sexy lyrics and dancing women with little clothes on. Words of most of these songs are degrading to women and sending out the wrong messages to our young people. How is this generation going to grow up, and what sort of morals and ideas are they going to have about the future of our world? Satan thinks he has this world in the palm of his hand, but he must think again. A spiritual war is going on, and we already know that Satan has lost. We are told in the book of Revelations that Satan and his followers will be cast into the lake of fire forever and ever.

Temptation, if we resist it, can strengthen us and bring us closer to our Lord. It can turn us into powerful men and women of God. Every time we fight against the Devil and we win, God sees this and he will reward us with more responsibility. The more we get tempted and fight temptation like soldiers of God's kingdom and destroy the enemy, the more powerful we become. So whenever you are confronted with temptation, look it in the eyes, grit your teeth together, and show it who's in control. Fight that Devil. He has no place in your life. Destroy him!

When we get tempted and give in to the Devil, we do not benefit in any way; we lose the fight. Giving in to temptation holds us back from the amazing life God has planned for us. God's power is there for us, and God won't let us be tempted beyond what we can handle. We have the Holy Spirit on our side; together with him we can fight whatever battle confronts us.

God warns us that we have to prepare ourselves as a warrior does before going into battle. A warrior would equip himself with his armor and shield to protect his body and a sword to fight the enemy. As God's children he expects us to be prepared to fight the Devil just like a warrior.

> *Finally, be strong in the Lord and in his great power. Put on the full armor of God so that you can fight against the devil's evil tricks. Our fight is not against people on earth but against the rulers and authorities and the powers of this world's darkness, against the spiritual powers of evil in the heavenly world. That is why you need to*

put on God's full armor. Then on the day
of evil you will be able to stand strong. And
when you have finished the whole fight, you
will still be standing. So stand strong, with
the belt of truth tied around your waist and
the protection of right living on your chest.
On your feet wear the Good News of peace
to help you stand strong. And also use the
shield of faith with which you can stop all
the burning arrows of the Evil One. Accept
God's salvation as your helmet, and take
the sword of the Spirit, which is the word of
God. (Ephesians 6:10–17 NCV)

Our guard against temptation is God's Word, the Bible, as a sword to protect ourselves, and the Holy Spirit to guide us. God has equipped us to protect ourselves with everything we need here on earth. Our Heavenly Father knows we have a tough enemy.

Like a Lion

Our enemy is like a lion waiting in the grass for that helpless, weak animal. He is like the lion that will sit and wait for hours watching a herd of wildebeests until he picks out the weakest one. Most likely he will attack the injured one or a baby that isn't equipped to help itself. As soon as he sets eyes on the prey he has purposely picked, the lion has found his lunch and there isn't much hope at all in stopping him. But we do have hope. God has given us his Spirit, who is our helper and our strength. We are never alone when we fight our battles. A battle or a temptation is never too strong that God hasn't given us sufficient strength and power to fight it.

> *Be self-controlled and alert. Your*
> *enemy the devil prowls around like a*
> *roaring lion looking for someone to devour.*
> (1 Peter 5:8 NIV 1984)

> *He lies in wait like a lion in cover; he*
> *lies in wait to catch the helpless; he catches*
> *the helpless and drags them off in his net.*
> (Psalm 10:9 NIV 1984)

New Christians are the easiest target for Satan to prey upon. A young, newborn Christian is not as equipped at protecting himself or knowing how to protect himself. Remember, when you were a tiny child, you couldn't defend yourself—your Mom and Dad were responsible for protecting you from any harm or danger. But every time you did hurt yourself or you were scared, the first thing you would do was to call out to Mom or Dad.

Likewise, God is our Heavenly Father, and we are to call to him in our need. He is always there for us and is always waiting for our call.

Believing in God is a wonderful start and the first step in your exciting journey with God. You may be unsure of what God expects of you and don't realize there is a lot more to God than just believing in him. If this sounds a little like yourself, you are the number one target for the Devil. The Devil doesn't want you to follow God or to know him as your Lord and Savior. You may have a little understanding about God and how to take your journey with God to the next step. Sins in your life are holding you back. You need to realize the importance of turning your back on these sinful things; doing so can become a matter of life or death. None of us know when our time on earth is done.

Satan deceives humans and tries to take away their right to seek freedom and truth. He shuts the door to their heart and locks it. He gives them science and unproven theories as to how the world was formed. He hardens their hearts and makes it look like Christians are the ones who are blinded, believing in no more than a detailed, far-fetched fairy tale. I am saddened when I hear people defend their unbelief in Christ. An atheist is someone who states that he doesn't believe in God and no divine purpose for humans exists. The atheist believes he is a product of an evolutionary process that has given him a large brain and self-awareness and that evolution has no ultimate objective other than the survival of the species.

This way of thinking is simply serving the Devil and letting him have complete control of your life, and you may not even know it. This might sound a little harsh, and I'm sorry, but it's true! You may think you are the one who is in control. You are not. The Devil wants you to think you are. Until you give God a chance to show you there is more to life with him, you will never understand. All you have to do is give him a try. What do you have to lose? You are not going to die from doing it. In fact you will find life. You can live your life in two ways. One is to serve Satan, and the other is to serve God. Until you decide to give your life to Jesus, you will always live life with the Devil. Satan doesn't want you to think any other way is possible.

Our world's history is based on Jesus and the events that happened in the Bible rather than on science and theories. Stop to think about our calendar system. We are living in the year 2012. What do you think this means? It is based on the life and death of Jesus Christ. We now live 2,012 years after the death of Jesus. When we speak of events before Jesus' time, we speak of the years Before Christ (BC). Today we are living in the years After Death (AD). I am amazed at how much our society today is based upon Biblical foundations, yet we have become so desensitized and oblivious to the truths of our history's foundation.

Jesus is everywhere you look; you just have to open your eyes and your heart to see it. Let the Holy Spirit speak to you now, and he will reveal himself to you. When you have an encounter with God, you can't deny his reality.

I often hear people say, "I don't know what this world is coming to." I know what the world is coming to. It's coming to a time of great trials and tribulation. The Devil and his angels and all the sinners will be cast into the Lake of Fire forever and ever. A new day is coming for those individuals who trust in the Lord Jesus. Jesus promised he would return to this earth and take all his children with him. Those who accept Jesus as their Lord and Savior will be taken to heaven. They will enter eternity with their Lord Jesus. That's where I'll be going, and I hope and pray that you also will be going there. The world as we know it is going to come to an end, and I believe the time is drawing near.

If you are reading this book today and you don't know whether you are going to heaven or hell, please continue on reading and make your decision to follow Jesus today.

CHAPTER 3

Heaven and Hell

As much as we do not like to think about death or the reality of what will happen to us when we die, at some time or another we have to face the fact that we will die, and we will spend eternity somewhere. For people who don't know Jesus, this subject is very uneasy. They are uncertain of what will happen to them and their loved ones. What if Christians are right and there is a hell?

In the beginning of time, when God created man on earth, he did not intend for us to die, because there was no need or purpose for humanity to die physically. His intent was to create man and woman to live on the earth, to walk and fellowship with God, and to inhabit the earth forever. However, because of what Satan did to Adam and Eve in the garden, sin entered the human race and corrupted God's plan. Sin destroyed God's desire to walk with us on earth and live in close fellowship with us because sin separates us from God.

God had a backup plan before the beginning of the earth. He knew that in order to get his children out of sin and to once again have his plan for us set right, he would have to bring death to the earth. Men and women would have to die physically in order to be with him forever. He would have to wipe out Satan, sin, and death. As a result, God created a lake of fire, which will burn forever.

God's plan of salvation through Jesus Christ now comes into play. God would send his only Son, Jesus to earth to become a sacrifice for us so that we will again be free from sin and free to live with our Father and Lord forever. When we believe in Jesus as our Lord, we become saved. Although we will still be faced with the physical death of our earthly bodies, we can rest assured that we will live on in new eternal bodies, in heaven with our Father and Lord forever.

For those who do not receive Jesus as their Lord and who choose not to follow him, they will face physical and spiritual death. When they die their physical death here on earth, they will not be given a second chance to become right with God; they will be separated from him forever in hell. Their eternal destiny will be certain death forever in the lake of fire.

So humans have two options: heaven and hell. When we think of eternity, then our lives here on earth seem very short in comparison. Eternity is a long time. Where do you think you would like to spend it?

When the Son of Man comes in his glory, and all the angels with him, he will sit on his glorious throne. All the nations will be gathered before him, and he will separate the people one from another as a shepherd separates the sheep from the goats. He will put the sheep on his right and the goats on his left.

Then the King will say to those on his right, "Come, you who are blessed by my Father; take your inheritance, the kingdom prepared for you since the creation of the world. For I was hungry and you gave me something to eat, I was thirsty and you gave me something to drink, I was a stranger and you invited me in, I needed clothes and you clothed me, I was sick and you looked after me, I was in prison and you came to visit me."

Then the righteous will answer him, "Lord, when did we see you hungry and feed you, or thirsty and give you something to drink? When did we see you a stranger and invite you in, or needing clothes and clothe you? When did we see you sick or in prison and go to visit you?"

The King will reply, "Truly I tell you, whatever you did for one of the least of these brothers and sisters of mine, you did for me."

Then he will say to those on his left, "Depart from me, you who are cursed, into the eternal fire prepared for the devil and his angels. For I was hungry and you gave me nothing to eat, I was thirsty and you gave me nothing to drink, I was a stranger and you did not invite me in, I needed clothes and you did not clothe me, I was sick and in prison and you did not look after me."

They also will answer, "Lord, when did we see you hungry or thirsty or a stranger or needing clothes or sick or in prison, and did not help you?"

> *He will reply, "Truly I tell you, whatever*
> *you did not do for one of the least of these,*
> *you did not do for me."*
>
> *Then they will go away to eternal*
> *punishment, but the righteous to eternal life.*
> (Matthew 25:31-46 NIV)

Heaven

Jesus said when he was on earth, "I am going to prepare a place for you." That place is heaven and where we will spend eternity with him.

Heaven is the place where our Father lives with his Son, Jesus, the Holy Spirit, and all the angels. It is also our home too, thanks to the sacrificial death of Jesus on the cross. Those of us who give our lives to Jesus and live according to his purpose have an eternal home and eternal rewards in heaven.

Heaven is God's eternal kingdom and a place more real than earth. It is a physical place with real streets, houses, grass and flowers, and rivers of water. When we get to heaven we will be in physical bodies, just as our bodies now are physical, but we will be given new bodies.

Everything in heaven is perfect. Heaven has no sickness, sadness, sin, or pain. We will be living how God intended us to live when he first created us, before the fall of man and before Adam and Eve sinned. Our purpose in heaven is to praise and worship God and to live in peace forever. He loves us so much that he wants to share eternity with us. He loves us just as much as he loves his Son, Jesus. When Jesus returns to collect us, we will be united with him forever.

Hell

Hell is the eternal place of the dead. Hell is a place of separation from God and separation from everyone else. When people joke and say that when they get to hell they will have a party with everyone there, they are very wrong. Hell allows no interaction. Although you will still have all your senses, emotions, and memory intact, you will have a body that is constantly being tortured, scared, and in pain. You will have the feeling of dying of thirst, of pain, and of torment, but in fact you won't be able to get out of that situation. It will be your reality for eternity.

Then I saw a great white throne and
him who was seated on it. The earth and the
heavens fled from his presence, and there was
no place for them. And I saw the dead, great

*and small, standing before the throne, and
books were opened. Another book was opened,
which is the book of life. The dead were judged
according to what they had done as recorded
in the books. The sea gave up the dead that
were in it, and death and Hades gave up the
dead that were in them, and each person was
judged according to what they had done. Then
death and Hades were thrown into the lake
of fire. The lake of fire is the second death.
Anyone whose name was not found written in
the book of life was thrown into the lake of fire.*
(Revelations 20:11–15 NIV)

After the eternal judgement, when God will judge all, if your name is not written in the book of life, which is in heaven, then your doom will be eternity in the lake of fire. The decision is final. You don't get a second chance. You can't get out. You never can subside the pain or the anguish.

I don't like to dwell on this for too long, but I do want you to be aware of it and know that you only have this life, here on earth, to get right with God, believe in Jesus, and have him as Lord and Savior. If you don't, and if you don't tell others about this reality, then the consequences are very bleak.

Remember you only have one chance, which is this life, here on earth. For some of you that small window of opportunity could be right here, right now, to make the decision that will affect how you will spend eternity. No one knows what tomorrow might bring.

CHAPTER 4

Jesus' Return and the End Times

The Lord himself will come down from heaven with a loud command, with the voice of the archangel, and with the trumpet call of God. And those who have died believing in Christ will rise first. After that, we who are still alive will be gathered up with them in the clouds to meet the Lord in the air. And we will be with the Lord forever.

(1 Thessalonians 4:16–17 NIV 1984)

That's right, someday soon the Lord Jesus will return to gather all his children, dead and alive. All the Christians will meet him in the air, and Jesus will take us out of this earth to be with him forever. This is called the *rapture*.

People who do not know Jesus or chose not to follow him with their whole hearts will be left behind on the earth. The earth will go into turmoil and despair, and darkness will cover the earth. It won't be a nice place to live after the second coming of Jesus. The Devil will take reign over the earth and will deceive many. The people left behind will be forced to receive a mark of the beast on their right hand or forehead. All who receive the mark will inevitably be selling their souls to the devil and forsaking God forever.

Many Christians including myself believe that the time of Jesus' return is near. The Bible states many things will happen on earth leading to his return and the end of the world as we know it. The Bible tells us that these two events are very closely linked by time. I am not going to go into too much detail about whether Jesus will return before, in the middle, or at the end of the end time events and tribulation, but I will tell you that both are going to happen, and we need to be ready. We need to fully live for God and love him above everything else. Those individuals who are still living in sin and are still caught up in worldly things will not be raptured; they will have to endure the great tribulation. As a result, you need to put aside anything that is holding you back from living a life without sin and gully committing your whole life to God.

Jesus warns us that no one except the Father knows the time when he will return for us. However, God does give us signs that the time is nearing. Matthew 24:26 (NIV 1984) says, "No one knows about that day or hour, not even the angels in heaven, nor the Son, but only the Father."

> *Therefore keep watch, because you do not know on what day your Lord will come. But understand this: If the owner of the house had known at what time of night the thief was coming, he would have kept watch and would not have let his house be broken into. So you also must be ready, because the Son of Man will come at an hour when you do not expect him.* (Matthew 24:42–44 NIV 1984)

The Bible gives many examples of signs that should warn us of the coming end of the age. Jesus gives six signs, Paul gives two, and the prophets give eleven others that will occur prior to soon after the end of the age. Although we are also told we will not know the time of the end, God obviously wanted us to know when that time was getting closer.

The Six Signs Jesus Gives to Indicate His Coming and the End of the Age

In Matthew 24:3 (NIV) Jesus was asked, "Tell us… when will this happen, and what will be the sign of your coming, and of the end of the age?" Jesus told his apostles to look for the following signs prior to his second coming and the end of the age.

1. False Prophets and Christs

Matthew 24:5 (NIV) tells us that "For many will come in my name, claiming, I am the Messiah, and will deceive many." Matthew 24:11 (NIV) also says, "And many false prophets will appear and deceive many people."

In the last several years many people have claimed to be the Messiah. These false prophets are a prelude to the ultimate false Christ, the Antichrist. Many New Age groups are anxiously awaiting the Antichrist, preparing the way for his acceptance as the head of the hierarchy of gods and the one who will usher in world peace.

2. Wars

Matthew 24:6 (NIV) states, "You will hear of wars and rumors of wars, but see to it that you are not alarmed. Such things must happen, but the end is still to come."

Rumors of wars in all areas of the world now occur frequently thanks to instant media coverage and the availability of a multitude of twenty-four–hour news sources.

Matthew 24:7 (NIV) says, "Nation will rise against nation, and kingdom against kingdom. There will be famines and earthquakes in various places. All these are the beginning of birth pains."

More people have been killed in warfare in this century than at any other time in history. Think of World Wars I and II, Korea, Vietnam, the Middle East, as well as the many genocides in this age. More and more countries work feverishly to develop devastating weapons of mass destruction. Add to that the expanding threat of terrorism and the potential for outbreak of war in so many nations and kingdoms across the globe.

3. Famines

We aren't strangers to the images that haunt our television sets, as we hear of the famine and starvation spreading across the African continent. However, the undernourished are not limited to Africa. A large portion of the world's 7 billion people suffers from a shortage of food and good nutrition.

4. Earthquakes

The number and intensity of earthquakes this century is at a level higher than any other time in history. A staggering number of seismic events occur around the world daily. By contrast, the years from 1890 to 1900 only had one major earthquake in the world.

In the last century the world has experienced the most horrific devastation and loss of life due to earthquakes. Haiti is still fresh in our minds, which took a staggering 316,000 lives. Another example is the earthquake in the Indian Ocean that caused the devastating Boxing Day tsunami in 2004, which claimed more than 230,000 lives. Recently, the earthquake in Christchurch, New Zealand, and the enormous quake that hit Japan causing destructive tsunamis and damaging the country's nuclear reactors.

5. Tribulations

Matthew 24:8–9 (NIV) says, "All these are the beginning of birth pains. Then you will be handed over to be persecuted and put to death, and you will be hated by all nations because of me."

Christians are under attack throughout the world today. In countries like Australia, United States, and the United Kingdom, Christians still enjoy freedom to worship God without suffering much more than ridicule, hatred, or discrimination at work and school. However in many other countries such as China, Sudan, Saudi Arabia, North Korea, Russia, and many Muslim nations, Christians suffer much greater persecution and often times death for their faith. During the tribulation this suffering will be worldwide and will continue even to the point of martyrdom. These first five signs will increase in intensity and severity as the tribulation approaches, much like the birth pangs or contractions of a pregnant woman worsen as the delivery time approaches.

6. The Gospel Will Be Preached Throughout the World

Matthew 24:14 (NIV) says, "And this gospel of the kingdom will be preached in the whole world as a testimony to all nations, and then the end will come."

This prophecy is already being fulfilled through television, radio, missionaries, the translation of the Bible into many languages, and the Internet. People all over the world now hear the message of Christ from missionaries who have the means to travel the globe, and via technology that allow us to communicate with people on the other side of the world right from our own homes, churches, and offices.

Two Characteristics of the End of the Age from the Apostle Paul

1. Godlessness in the Last Days

But mark this: There will be terrible times in the last days. People will be lovers of themselves, lovers of money, boastful, proud, abusive, disobedient to their parents, ungrateful, unholy, without love, unforgiving, slanderous, without self-control, brutal, not lovers of the good, treacherous, rash, conceited, lovers of pleasure rather than lovers of God—having a form of godliness but denying its power. Have nothing to do with such people.

They are the kind who worm their way into homes and gain control over gullible women, who are loaded down with sins and are swayed by all kinds of evil desires, always learning but never able to come to a knowledge of the truth. (2 Timothy 3:1–7 NIV)

For anyone who has watched television, read a newspaper, lost a retirement to corporate greed and corruption, or just walked outside their front door, this prophecy obviously has been fulfilled by our generation. Our leaders are often corrupt; our cities are filled with crime, brutality, and neon signs proclaiming our sinful, godless nature. The New Age Movement brings in increasing numbers of mystics who claim to be the enlightened ones. They are some of the most educated and influential people in our societies and yet the most lacking in real truth.

2. Falling Away from the Faith

In the presence of God and of Christ Jesus, who will judge the living and the dead, and in view of his appearing and his kingdom, I give you this charge:

Preach the word; be prepared in season and out of season; correct, rebuke and encourage—with great patience and careful instruction. For the time will come when people will not put up with sound doctrine. Instead, to suit their own desires, they will gather around them a great number of teachers to say what their itching ears want to hear. (2 Timothy 4:1–3 NIV)

Churches today are becoming more and more pleasing to what people want to hear. Some even are embracing New Age interfaith agenda and denying Christ as the only way to salvation. Giving in to the politically correct media and a corrupt society, some have embraced homosexuality as an acceptable alternate lifestyle and preach tolerance and compromise in place of God's truth for the salvation of the world. The environmentalist movement within the New Age movement lures people into worship of mother earth and belief in past lives, reincarnation, and karma.

The Anti-Christ and the Mark of the Beast

In the end times Satan will take up his throne on earth in the body of the Antichrist. He will falsely resemble Jesus and deceive the world into world peace. Those who receive the mark of the beast will be under his control. This mark will be forced on everyone, either on their right hand or on their forehead. The Bible warns that whoever receives the mark of the beast will be Satan's forever with no turning back from their decision to follow him. Those people will ultimately spend eternity in the lake of fire.

> *If anyone worships the beast and his*
> *image and receives his mark on the forehead*
> *or on the hand, he, too, will drink of the*
> *wine of God's fury, which has been poured*
> *full strength into the cup of his wrath.*
> (Revelation 14:9–10 NIV 1984)

People who refuse the mark will receive severe penalties, and those who get it will receive great rewards. The Bible tells us that without the mark people won't be able to buy or sell, which suggests that it is a type of currency or access to purchasing. Thinking about this mark is very scary, but we are God's children and he has told us that he will never leave or forsake us. We may go through a difficult period, but in the end we will spend eternity with him in heaven. And as I said before, no one knows the hour that Jesus will come for us. We may not have to endure all the tribulation of the end of the world. Jesus can return to take us to be with him at any time.

The key here is to be ready. Live your life expecting Jesus to return at any moment. Make every day count. Make sure you are living fully for God and not for the world. Ask God to show you the things in your life that he doesn't like and be free from sin. Pray and ask for strength to overcome your trials. Read your Bible, listen for God's voice, and never give up.

CHAPTER 5

Judgment Day

Judgment Day is the final and eternal judgment by God of all people. It will take place after the resurrection of the dead and the second coming of Christ. It will be the end of time and the beginning of eternity. It is a day that everyone who has ever lived will stand in front of God. The unbelievers of Christ will be judged guilty of their sin and will be cast into the lake of fire prepared for Satan and his angels. The believers' judgment will be very different. It will be a time when God recognizes all the good and eternal deeds they have done. He will reward those individuals who followed him and who showed love and compassion to others. He will thank them and say, "Well done, good and faithful servant. Thank you."

He answered, "The one who sowed the good seed is the Son of Man. The field is the world, and the good seed stands for the people of the kingdom. The weeds are the people of the evil one, and the enemy who sows them is the devil. The harvest is the end of the age, and the harvesters are angels.

"As the weeds are pulled up and burned in the fire, so it will be at the end of the age. The Son of Man will send out his angels, and they will weed out of his kingdom everything that causes sin and all who do evil. They will throw them into the blazing furnace, where there will be weeping and gnashing of teeth. Then the righteous will shine like the sun in the kingdom of their Father. Whoever has ears, let them hear. (Matthew 13:37–43 NIV)

The Lord will clearly judge us on the works we have done on earth. We are judged on the obedience of his commandments and the fruit that we produce. The Bible has many commandments to love one another and laws of righteous living. Jesus' life is a testimony of how we should also live. We, as believers, are to live in accordance with God's commandments and his will or purpose for our life. God has written each one of us a book on how he created us to live, in accordance with our time, our gifts, talents, and unique purpose in the kingdom. If we live contrary to our purpose, or are not obedient to God's commands, then we may not receive our full reward in heaven. That's why seeking and asking God your purpose is important. We need to be living every day in God's will and living out our purpose. If you are unsure what your purpose is, you need to ask God for direction. He will speak to you.

> *Then I saw a great white throne and*
> *him who was seated on it. The earth and the*
> *heavens fled from his presence, and there was*
> *no place for them. And I saw the dead, great*
> *and small, standing before the throne, and*
> *books were opened. Another book was opened,*
> *which is the book of life. The dead were judged*
> *according to what they had done as recorded*
> *in the books.* (Revelation 20:11–12 NIV)

The Book of Life is a very real book. Those of us who obey God and accept Jesus as our Savior are written in the Book of Life. Those whose name is not written in the Book of Life will face a fiery existence in the lake of fire.

> *The Lord All-Powerful says, "Then I will*
> *come to you and judge you. I will be quick*
> *to testify against those who take part in evil*
> *magic, adultery, and lying under oath, those*

> *who cheat workers of their pay and who*
> *cheat widows and orphans, those who are*
> *unfair to foreigners, and those who do not*
> *respect me."* (Malachi 3:5 NCV)

We only have one chance, and that is this life here and now. After that, our time is up; we will have to face what is coming to us, either good or bad. Let this make us aware of how we live our lives each day. Each day has in it the opportunities to affect how we will spend eternity. Let's make each minute count toward the day when our Lord will say to us, "Well done, good and faithful servant."

I pray that you will make your decisions wisely, so you will never hear, "Depart from me, I never knew you."

CHAPTER 6

God's Plan for Your Life

Teach us how short our lives really are so that we can be wise ...

Lord our God, treat us well.

Give us success in what we do;

yes, give us success in what we do.

(Psalm 90:12, 17 NCV)

When God designed us, he had a plan and purpose for us. He didn't just randomly throw us into existence in any country with any family in any time in history. He designed us specifically for this time, specifically for this place and specifically for this purpose. God is not a random God. He has everything placed in its correct order for such a time, such a place, and such a purpose. If we live according to God's plan for our lives, then we can rest assured that we are exactly where God intends us to be. If we put God first and seek him, he will direct our path.

Jeremiah 29:11 (NIV) says, "'For I know the plans I have for you,' declares the LORD, 'plans to prosper you and not to harm you, plans to give you hope and a future.'"

We can be sure that the plans and purpose God has for us are plans to prosper us and give us a great future, not to harm us. We are God's beloved children, and he will not give his children bad things.

> *Which of you, if your son asks for*
> *bread, will give him a stone? Or if he*
> *asks for a fish, will give him a snake? If*
> *you, then, though you are evil, know how*
> *to give good gifts to your children, how*
> *much more will your Father in heaven*
> *give good gifts to those who ask him!*
> (Matthew 7:9–11 NIV)

Determining your purpose for your life is not rocket science. It is not meant to confuse you. If you are confused and unsure, ask God. He will not hold back from telling you your purpose. As long as whatever you do, you do it for the sake of blessing God and others, you have no alarm to panic. God will soon tell you if what you are doing is outside his will for your life. He will show you signs that what you are doing is not in line with his plan.

On one occasion an expert in the law stood up to test Jesus. "Teacher," he asked, "what must I do to inherit eternal life?"

"What is written in the Law?" he replied. "How do you read it?"

He answered, "'Love the Lord your God with all your heart and with all your soul and with all your strength and with all your mind'; and, 'Love your neighbour as yourself.'"

"You have answered correctly," Jesus replied. "Do this and you will live."

But he wanted to justify himself, so he asked Jesus, "And who is my neighbour?"

In reply Jesus said: "A man was going down from Jerusalem to Jericho, when he was attacked by robbers. They stripped him of his clothes, beat him and went away,

*leaving him half dead. A priest happened
to be going down the same road, and when
he saw the man, he passed by on the other
side. So too, a Levite, when he came to the
place and saw him, passed by on the other
side. But a Samaritan, as he travelled,
came where the man was; and when he saw
him, he took pity on him. He went to him
and bandaged his wounds, pouring on oil
and wine. Then he put the man on his own
donkey, brought him to an inn and took care
of him. The next day he took out two denarii
and gave them to the innkeeper. 'Look after
him,' he said, 'and when I return, I will
reimburse you for any extra expense you
may have.'*

*"Which of these three do you think was a
neighbour to the man who fell into the hands
of robbers?"*

*The expert in the law replied, "The one
who had mercy on him."*

Jesus told him, "Go and do likewise."
(Luke 10:25–37 NIV)

We see here that God desires us to love him with our whole being and to love others as we love ourselves. Every day we have many opportunities where we can love and do good to others. But how often do we turn a blind eye to someone in need, and think someone else will take care of it? It is our will to help our neighbour and to make a difference in someone's life. Love is a fruit of the Spirit, and the evidence that we love God and are living out our purpose through his Holy Spirit is in our fruit.

We are told to love God and obey him in all we do. He has set up guidelines for us to live by. Part of our purpose in life is to obey God and live righteously. Doing so pleases God, and he rewards us for honoring him.

Jesus told us to go out into the world and spread the good news of the Gospel. This is also our purpose. We are to continue Jesus' mission and purpose by telling others about his love and salvation. We are to share Jesus with our family, our friends, and our neighbours. We are to spread the Gospel to the whole earth.

God has created us each with individual gifts and talents. Some of us are good at some things better than others. We each have something special to give and to share with the world. Some people are gifted in music, and others are gifted in speaking. Some are created to be successful in business, and others are crafty in the arts and entertainment. Whatever it is that you have a passion for and are good at, you have a purpose in that arena. As long as what you do with your life feels right and can be used to bless others and bless the Lord, then you can be sure that what you are doing is purposeful in the Kingdom of God.

God created and designed us for relationship with him. This is his desire and it should be ours as well. Nothing pleases God more than us having close relationship with him. It is our purpose to love, honor, and abide in him. He is so close to us, he lives inside of us. All we need to do is open our eyes and heart and realize the reality of his love for us. He loves us so much he planned us before the world was spoken into existence. He designed us for our special purpose in his Kingdom. He made us out of the dust of the earth so he could have a relationship with us and be his children forever. That's how much he wanted us!

When Adam messed up God's plan and fell into sin and was separated from God in the garden of Eden, God had another plan to recover his precious children. He planned to send his only Son, Jesus, to earth to be a sacrifice for our sin. Only through the death and resurrection of Jesus are we able to walk in harmony with our Heavenly Father. He took every measure to get us back, but we have a choice. We can choose to take hold of his hand or to turn our backs and be separated from him forever. The choice is all ours.

Most importantly it is our purpose to tell others about his incredible love. Without the opportunity, many will not know God. It is now up to us to spread the good news and to give others the opportunity to know their Father. Don't keep this to yourself. One day you will be judged and an eternal destiny will await you. What you do today and all the days on this earth will determine the rewards you receive in eternity.

CHAPTER 7

Salvation

I will judge you, each one according to his
ways, declares the Sovereign Lord. Repent!
Turn away from all your offenses; then sin will
not be your downfall. Rid yourselves of all the
offenses you have committed, and get a new
heart and a new spirit ... Repent and live!'
(Ezekiel 18:30–32 NIV 1984)

Salvation is the divine providence of God's children from spiritual death by providing them with an eternal life. Salvation is the deliverance from sin and its effects.

Our Salvation is made possible by the life, death, and resurrection of Jesus Christ. Jesus took God's justice and wrath upon himself and was crushed in order to conquer death and bring into right standing with God, those who believe and repent.

As John 3:16 (NIV 1984) says, "For God so loved the world that he gave his one and only Son, that whoever believes in him shall not perish but have eternal life."

Only through Jesus and his willingness to fulfill his Father's purpose may we have access to salvation. Salvation is a free gift from God; anyone who chooses to receive it shall be saved from their sin and enter into eternal life. Through salvation we have access to God's grace and power. Jesus gave us his life and death so that we can have eternal life with our Father in heaven. Because of the obedience and fulfillment of Jesus' purpose, he now sits at the right hand of the Father on the throne. Jesus is our Lord and our Savior.

Good works cannot save us. We need to receive salvation through Jesus Christ to be saved. I hope this book has been a helpful tool for you to get to know the truths about God, Christianity, Satan, your destiny, and ultimately, your salvation.

I know it might be a lot to digest, but take your time and reread over chapters if you need to. This is the most important information you could ever read. Jesus wants to save you from your sins, and he is waiting to offer you eternal life. It is free; all you need to do is to ask, believe, and then receive. If you pray the prayer below and are seriously willing to give Jesus a chance, I promise that you will be making the best decision of your life.

"Dear Lord,

I admit I am a sinner, and I understand that good works alone will not get me entry into heaven or eternal life. Forgive me for my sins and cleanse me from all my wrong doing. Thank you for sending your only Son, Jesus, to earth to die and be a sacrifice for my sins. I believe that what you say is true, and that Jesus is the only way to true life. I believe he died and rose again for my salvation, and I accept him as my only Lord and Savior. I give you my life, and I give you my soul and my heart. I want to live my life for you and your kingdom. Show me your purpose for my life, and give me understanding and wisdom. Protect me from evil and lead me on the road to everlasting life. Cleanse me with the blood of Jesus and send me your Holy Spirit to be my helper and teacher. Thank you that I am now your precious child, and thank you for writing my name in the Book of Life. I trust you, and I will live my life for you.

In Jesus' Name I pray,
Amen."

I would like to welcome you to the family of God. The decision you made today will affect you for the rest of eternity. I am so thankful that you have had the opportunity to read this book and receive salvation.

Get yourself a Bible and read it every day. It is God's Word. Talk to the person who gave you this book. If he or she is a Christian, that person will help you on your journey. Get into a Bible-based church or meet regularly with other believers. Doing so will strengthen you and help keep you from stumbling. Remember that Satan is out to get you; be aware of his temptation and his attacks. Never forget that you have Jesus living in you and the Holy Spirit to help you and guide you. Have faith, and you will possess the same power that Jesus had when he was on earth. Grace is free for you, and through it you have the power to overcome anything. Pray, and talk to God. He desires to have a close relationship with you. Ask for everything in Jesus' name, and he says he will give it to you. Have faith when you pray, and believe that God will provide for you. Remember, faith is the access to power and grace. You have that within you, it is real, and you can be sure that if you are living in the purpose of God, you will be given everything you need.

You are now born again, and God has made you a new creation. The old has gone and the new has come. Your motives and desires will change. The sinful things you once enjoyed won't matter anymore. You will receive new desires and a new heart.

Telling as many people as possible about Jesus is important. Time is running out, and we don't know how long we have left until his return. We must fulfill our purpose and spread the good news to others who do not yet know. For someday soon our God will judge us, and the eternal destinies of our unsaved friends and family will be upon our heads. I would not like for God to ask me, "Why didn't you tell them about me?"

I know Christianity is sometimes a difficult topic to bring up, which is why I wrote this book. Use this book as a tool to spread the good news and to let others know the truth. Give a copy to your friends, family, neighbours, and coworkers. Spread the good news and don't delay. The time is near that our Savior will return. Now is the time for us to be ready. Let us be confident that we have done all we can to provide the key to unlock the door to the hearts of our unsaved brothers and sisters. They need to know the truth too. Make this your mission today.

May God bless you in your journey.

Father's Heart

"Two thousand years ago, my Son, Jesus,
the one who shaped the universe and formed
the earth, was slain in a painful death.

He carried the pain and suffering for my
dear children who couldn't save themselves
from the vultures of this world.

My pain is now for my children. My
children must come to me and trust me. I
am a loving God: I hear all prayers and am
always listening to my little ones' needs.

I have what it takes to heal you. I am all-powerful
and all-knowing. I am your God and your Father.

My heart pains, and I am gripped with sorrow
for my children. They have turned their backs
on me. They have walked away from what is
righteous and walk in their own understanding.

How foolish!

Do they not know the good things I have for them?
Have they stopped reading the scriptures that bring
life? Have they lost all understanding of my promises?

They need not walk alone. They need not be
tormented and hindered. They do not see they are
walking straight into the fiery depths of hell.

There is no freedom in walking alone.
There is danger at every turn. I see my
creation dying. I watch them by the thousands
being led through the gates of hell.

I cry in front of my angels. They know
my pain and sorrow. They remained with
me when I sent my Son to the depths.

They understand the price of salvation.
They trusted me and continued to serve me.
They please me and make my heart rejoice.

They did not wonder off, as many did. They
will remain with me for all eternity. They were
wise and trusted me. They knew my promises
and saw the great things I have done.

*Their hope is to see my children home with me.
My Holy Hosts are excited for the return of the Saints.*

*Open your eyes and your hearts. I am not far
from you. I have not turned and left you. I have
always been here. I have good things for you.*

Trust me."

~ Your Heavenly Father ~

About the Author

*E*rin Reid grew up in a small sea side town in Tasmania, Australia. She has a passion for helping people discover their full potential in life. Erin has acquired biblical knowledge and wisdom through her own personal relationship with her Creator. In her youth she enjoyed being a counsellor at holiday camps, and developed a passion for working with children and young people. Now, a wife and a new mother, she enjoys spending time with her family, reading, and walks along the beach. Erin and her family now live in tropical North Queensland, Australia.

For information on the author, questions and feedback visit www.unlockthedoor.com.au.